Paradigm Shift: Reform or Rough Terrain Ahead

Relive and Imagine 2014 to 2029

Aditya Sharma

INDIA • SINGAPORE • MALAYSIA

ISBN 979-8-89446-524-1

Contents

Foreword 5

Introduction 7

1. JAM Trinity 9
2. LPG Cylinders and Electricity Coverage Pan India 15
3. Silence in Pakistan and Astonishment in China 21
4. Conquering Article 370 27
5. Ram Mandir 33
6. Revolution in Defence Infrastructure and Global Exports 39
7. Increasing World Stature & Multiple War Evacuation 45
8. Fight against Malnutrition 51
9. Lifting AFSPA from All Regions 57
10. Making Naxalism and Northeast Issues History 63
11. Women Reservation Act, 2023 71
12. Infrastructure Revamp Across Sectors 75
13. Uniform Civil Code 81
14. One Nation One Election 87
15. Opposition's Struggle 93

Synopsis 97

Epilogue 99

About the Author 101

Foreword

Hello there,

I'm thrilled to share a little piece of my world – a book my husband wrote. You see, he's not just any author; he's a man who lives and breathes world and Indian politics with a heart as big as the global challenges.

Throughout our conversations, arguments, and moments of deep understanding, I've realised just how deeply he cares about what's happening out there. He's not merely spouting facts; he's sharing stories of real people, their struggles, and their triumphs.

This book isn't solely about politics; it's about change and how change has happened throughout the country. It's about understanding Indian development through the eyes of those often overlooked. And trust me, there's something incredibly powerful about viewing India through that lens.

So, if you're like me, someone who's always trying to make sense of the chaos around us, I urge you to pick up this book. Let it take you on a journey of discovery, empathy, and perhaps even a little hope.

With love,

Shubhangi Sharma
(MBA, LLB)

Introduction

In the annals of Indian political history, the period from 2014 to 2029 will be marked by seismic shifts, transformative reforms, and unprecedented decisions. As the pages of our nation's story unfolded, the spotlight illuminated moments of triumph, controversy, and resilience. In this book, we embark on a journey through the corridors of power, tracing the evolution of governance and the impact of policy decisions on the fabric of our society. The merry-go-round of the opposition keeps an individual at the centre of all its criticism rather than the government and its policies.

The dawn of the 21st century brought renewed optimism and ambition for India's future. The government's visionary initiatives, propelled by the mantra of "Sabka Saath, Sabka Vikas," aimed to empower every citizen and usher in an era of inclusive growth. From the inception of the JAM (Jan Dhan-Aadhaar-Mobile) initiative to the expansion of LPG and electricity coverage, the first phase of our narrative reflects on the efforts to bridge the gap between aspiration and reality.

As the political landscape evolved, the government's mantra also evolved and now become "Sabka Sath, Sabka Vikas, Sabka Vishwas. Along with this, the challenges facing the nation also kept growing. One of the many challenges the government took on was the decision to abrogate Article 370 in Jammu and Kashmir, the historic verdict on the Ayodhya dispute, and the push for defence infrastructure development underscored the government's resolve to tackle entrenched issues head-on. Yet, each reform was met with fierce opposition, sparking nationwide debates. The courts quashed some opposition, and public acceptance of such major policy reforms quashed others.

Looking ahead, the chapters hereon offer a glimpse into the future trajectory of our nation. The government now has another feather in its flock, "Sabka Sath, Sabka Vikas, Sabka Vishwas, Sabka Prayas". From the ambitious goal of ending malnutrition and insurgency to the imperative of women's empowerment. To see the end of AFSPA and the massive infrastructure revamp to increase ease of living, we explore the aspirations and decisions that will shape the next chapter of India's journey. From aiming to fulfil the long-standing promise of the Constitution of UCC to returning to the One Nation One Election, all these are a recipe for strong, decisive and bold steps, which this government has previously shown the gumpsum to go ahead with.

Through meticulous research, candid anecdotes, and insightful analysis, this book seeks to capture the essence of a nation in transition—a nation grappling with its past, navigating its present, and envisioning its future. A nation where the opposition wasted a decade targeting an individual rather than a government or its policies. This is a nation wherein the opposition of the day is not used to being in opposition and, hence, is meticulously failing at it. Join us as we unravel the complexities of governance the good governance reform, and delve into the heart of India's democratic experiment.

JAM Trinity

The inception of the JAM (Jan Dhan-Aadhaar-Mobile) Initiative

In August 2014, the Indian government embarked on a bold journey to revolutionise the country's financial landscape by introducing the JAM initiative. JAM, an acronym for Jan Dhan-Aadhaar-Mobile, was designed to link three critical elements: bank accounts (Jan Dhan), biometric identification (Aadhaar), and mobile phones. The initiative aimed to promote financial inclusion and empower citizens through digital connectivity.

The inception of JAM was driven by the realisation that despite India's burgeoning economy, a significant portion of the population remained unbanked and financially excluded. The government recognised that addressing this gap was crucial for inclusive growth and economic empowerment. By integrating bank accounts with Aadhaar and mobile numbers, the JAM initiative sought to create a seamless digital infrastructure that efficiently delivers financial services and social benefits.

The cornerstone of the JAM initiative was the ambitious task of linking bank accounts, Aadhaar cards, and mobile phone numbers. The Pradhan Mantri Jan Dhan Yojana (PMJDY), launched as part of the initiative, aimed to provide every household with a bank account. By May 2024, over 520 million Jan Dhan accounts had been opened, marking a significant step towards financial inclusion.

Aadhaar, India's biometric identification system, played a pivotal role in verifying the identity of account holders. With over 1.27 billion people enrolled, Aadhaar provided a robust framework for linking individuals to their bank accounts and mobile numbers. This integration facilitated direct benefit transfers (DBTs), ensuring that subsidies and welfare payments reached the intended beneficiaries without intermediaries.

Mobile phones, the third pillar of JAM, acted as a conduit for financial transactions and communication. With over a billion mobile subscribers, the potential for digital financial services was immense. Mobile banking and payment applications leveraged this connectivity to bring banking services to the fingertips of millions.

Need for Financial Inclusion and Digital Empowerment

Financial inclusion is more than just access to a bank account; it encompasses the availability and usage of a full suite of financial services, including savings, credit, insurance, and remittances. For years, large segments of the Indian population were excluded from formal financial systems, particularly in rural areas. This exclusion limited their ability to save securely, access credit, and receive social benefits.

The JAM initiative aimed to break down these barriers by leveraging technology to create an inclusive financial ecosystem. Digital empowerment through JAM was envisioned to drive economic growth, reduce poverty, and enhance the standard of living for millions of Indians.

Opposition's Scepticism and Concerns

Despite its ambitious goals, the JAM initiative faced scepticism and opposition from various quarters. Critics raised concerns about privacy and data security, fearing that the centralised nature of Aadhaar could lead to misuse of personal information. There were also apprehensions about the feasibility of implementing such a vast project, especially in remote areas with limited digital infrastructure.

Opposition parties questioned the government's ability to safeguard the data of millions of citizens and ensure that the benefits reached the truly needy. Concerns about excluding marginalised communities, who might not have easy access to Aadhaar or mobile phones, were also highlighted.

However, the opposition's approach to these concerns often lacked depth and consistency. While they raised valid points about data breaches, such as those involving Aadhaar data leaks on the dark web, their efforts to hold the government accountable were sporadic and lacked concrete follow-up. For instance, despite multiple instances of Aadhaar data leaks, the opposition did not effectively push for stronger data protection laws or comprehensive cybersecurity measures. They also failed to present a unified front or a clear alternative strategy that could address these vulnerabilities more effectively.

Anecdote Illustrating the Impact of Financial Inclusion

Consider the story of Sangeeta, a small farmer from a remote village in Uttar Pradesh. Before the JAM initiative, Sangeeta struggled to access credit and relied on local moneylenders who charged exorbitant interest rates. With the opening of a Jan Dhan account linked to her Aadhaar and mobile number, Sangeeta could now receive direct benefit transfers from government schemes, access affordable credit from formal institutions, and save securely.

This transformation empowered Sangeeta to invest in better farming techniques, increase her yield, and improve her family's living standards.

Her story is just one of millions illustrating the profound impact of financial inclusion driven by the JAM initiative.

Visible Transformation: Increased Financial Access and Reduced Leakages

The visible transformation brought about by the JAM initiative is evident in several key areas:

1. Increased Financial Access: By 2024, the number of bank accounts opened under the PMJDY exceeded 520 million, significantly increasing financial access for the previously unbanked population. Women accounted for 56% of these account holders, highlighting the initiative's role in empowering women economically.
2. Reduced Leakages: Direct benefit transfers linked to Aadhaar helped reduce leakages and corruption in subsidy disbursement. The government estimated savings of over $12 billion due to reduced fraud and efficient delivery of subsidies.
3. Enhanced Digital Payments: The integration of mobile phones facilitated the growth of digital payments. The Unified Payments Interface (UPI), launched in 2016, saw exponential growth, with monthly transactions surpassing 1 billion by 2019.

Examples from Other Nations

India's JAM initiative is not unique in its goals; several other nations have undertaken similar efforts to enhance financial inclusion through digital means. However, the scale and integration of the JAM initiative make it distinct. Here are some examples of financial inclusion efforts in other countries:

- Kenya: M-Pesa, a mobile phone-based money transfer service launched in 2007, revolutionised financial inclusion in Kenya. By 2019, over 80% of the adult population used M-Pesa, enabling secure transactions and access to financial services in areas lacking traditional banking infrastructure. However, M-Pesa primarily focuses on mobile money transfers and lacks the comprehensive integration seen in India's JAM.
- Brazil: The Bolsa Família programme, initiated in 2003, uses digital payments to assist low-income families financially. The programme's integration with banking services has improved the efficiency of benefit distribution and reduced poverty. While Bolsa Família has successfully reduced poverty, its scope is limited to social assistance and does not encompass JAM's broader financial inclusion objectives.
- China: The rapid adoption of mobile payment platforms like Alipay and WeChat Pay has driven financial inclusion in China. By leveraging digital technology, these platforms have brought banking services to millions, particularly in rural areas. However, China's approach is heavily market-driven and lacks the centralised coordination of JAM, which integrates government welfare schemes directly with financial services.

The JAM initiative stands out globally for its comprehensive approach, scale, and government-driven integration. Here is how it compares and often surpasses other international efforts:

1. Comprehensive Integration: Unlike M-Pesa, which focuses mainly on mobile money transfers, JAM integrates banking, identification, and mobile connectivity, creating a more holistic financial ecosystem.
2. Government-Driven and Inclusive: Unlike the market-driven approaches in China, JAM is a government-driven initiative

aimed at inclusivity. It ensures that even the most marginalised populations are brought into the financial fold, leveraging government welfare schemes to drive inclusion.

3. Broad Scope and Scale: While Bolsa Família in Brazil focuses on social assistance, JAM covers a broader scope, including financial transactions, savings, credit, insurance, and subsidies, all integrated within a massive scale, addressing over 1.2 billion individuals.
4. Direct Benefit Transfers: JAM's Direct Benefit Transfer mechanism, facilitated through Aadhaar and Jan Dhan accounts, significantly reduces leakages and ensures that subsidies reach the intended beneficiaries, an area where many global programmes fall short.
5. Digital Empowerment: By linking mobile phones with bank accounts and Aadhaar, JAM enhances digital financial literacy and empowerment, driving the adoption of digital payment systems like UPI.

The JAM initiative is a testament to how a well-coordinated, government-led programme can achieve massive financial inclusion and digital empowerment, setting a benchmark for other nations to follow.

LPG Cylinders and Electricity Coverage Pan India

Ensuring every household has access to basic amenities like clean cooking fuel and reliable electricity has been a monumental challenge in India. For decades, millions of Indians, particularly in rural areas, depended on traditional biomass fuels such as wood and cow dung for cooking. This dependence posed severe health risks due to indoor air pollution. Simultaneously, the lack of reliable electricity hindered educational and economic activities, severely affecting the quality of life.

Recognising these critical issues, the Indian government, under Prime Minister Narendra Modi's leadership, launched ambitious initiatives to expand LPG (liquefied petroleum gas) and electricity coverage nationwide. The aim was not merely to provide these utilities but to address broader issues of energy poverty and improve the living standards for millions of Indians.

The idea of Ensuring Clean Cooking Fuel and Electricity Access

Pradhan Mantri Ujjwala Yojana (PMUY): Launched in May 2016, PMUY aimed to provide LPG connections to women from Below Poverty Line (BPL) households. By March 2024, over 103 million LPG connections had been distributed, significantly increasing the penetration of clean cooking fuel in rural India. This initiative replaced traditional cooking fuels with cleaner alternatives, thereby reducing health risks associated with indoor air pollution.

Saubhagya Scheme (Pradhan Mantri Sahaj Bijli Har Ghar Yojana): Launched in September 2017, this scheme aimed to achieve universal household electrification. By March 2019, the government announced the electrification of 100% of households, covering over 26 million homes. This milestone was a significant achievement in ensuring that even the most remote villages received reliable electricity.

Reforms Needed to Eliminate Energy Poverty After 75 Years of Independence

Despite 75 years of independence, a significant portion of India's population continued to live in energy poverty. The PMUY and Saubhagya schemes were pivotal in addressing this issue, but several reforms were necessary to ensure sustainable and equitable energy access:

1. Infrastructure Development: Building and upgrading infrastructure to ensure reliable electricity supply and LPG distribution networks, especially in remote and difficult terrains. For instance, the government laid over 365,000 km of power transmission lines to improve grid connectivity.
2. Subsidies and Financial Support: Providing financial incentives and subsidies to make LPG and electricity affordable for low-income households. The government allocated over ₹1.2 lakh crore for the PMUY and ensured beneficiaries received a subsidy directly in their bank accounts.
3. Awareness Campaigns: Conducting awareness programmes to educate the populace about the benefits of clean energy and encouraging the adoption of LPG and electricity.

4. Monitoring and Maintenance: Establishing robust monitoring systems to ensure infrastructure maintenance and uninterrupted supply of electricity and LPG.

Opposition's Criticism and Lack of Legislative Action

While the initiatives received widespread acclaim, they were not without criticism. Opposition parties raised concerns about the implementation and sustainability of these programmes. Critics argued that the schemes were politically motivated and timed to gain favour among voters in the run-up to elections. There were also concerns about the financial burden on the exchequer and the long-term viability of the subsidies.

One significant concern was the security of Aadhaar data linked to the Direct Benefit Transfer (DBT) scheme. Multiple data leak incidents on the dark web raised questions about the adequacy of data protection measures. Despite these concerns, the opposition struggled to pin the government on these issues due to their lack of a cohesive strategy or legislative action to address and improve the existing framework.

Anecdote Highlighting the Benefits of Clean Energy Access

Consider the story of Meera, a resident of a small village in Bihar. Before receiving an LPG connection under the PMUY scheme, Meera spent hours collecting firewood and suffered from chronic respiratory issues due to indoor air pollution. The introduction of LPG transformed her daily life. Cooking became easier and healthier, and she had more time to devote to her family and other productive activities. Similarly, the arrival of electricity in her village under the

Saubhagya scheme allowed her children to study at night and opened new avenues for economic activities, improving the family's overall quality of life.

Visible Transformation: Improved Living Standards and Health Outcomes

The visible transformation brought about by the expansion of LPG and electricity coverage in India is multifaceted:

1. Health Benefits: The transition from traditional biomass fuels to LPG has significantly reduced indoor air pollution, leading to better respiratory health and decreased morbidity, especially among women and children. According to a World Health Organisation (WHO) report, indoor air pollution causes over 1 million deaths annually in India; initiatives like PMUY are critical in reducing this number.
2. Economic Opportunities: Reliable electricity has enabled small businesses to thrive, boosted agricultural productivity through better irrigation facilities, and provided new employment opportunities in rural areas. The Rural Electrification Corporation (REC) reported a 40% increase in rural enterprises post-electrification.
3. Educational Advancements: Electrification has allowed students to study after dark, leading to better educational outcomes and future opportunities. The Saubhagya scheme alone facilitated electricity access to over 200 million people, significantly impacting educational activities.
4. Women's Empowerment: Access to LPG has freed women from the time-consuming task of collecting firewood, allowing them to

pursue education, work, and other activities. According to a study by the International Energy Agency (IEA), access to modern energy services improves women's health, reduces their workload, and enhances their economic productivity.

World Examples of Large-Scale Gas Cylinder or Electricity Distribution

While the scale and integration of India's initiatives are unparalleled, other countries have also implemented large-scale energy distribution programmes:

- Kenya: The Last Mile Connectivity Project aims to connect all households to the national grid, enhancing economic growth and reducing poverty. By 2019, the project had connected over 2.5 million households.
- Brazil: The Luz Para Todos programme has successfully electrified remote rural areas, improving living standards and economic activities. Since its inception in 2003, the programme has connected over 16 million people to the grid.
- China: China's extensive electrification programmes have reached even the most remote areas, contributing to the country's rapid economic development. By 2015, China had achieved 100% electrification, impacting over 40 million rural residents.

The expansion of LPG and electricity coverage under the Modi government between 2014 and 2019 has been a transformative initiative, touching the lives of millions of Indians. These programmes have significantly improved living standards and fostered socio-economic development by addressing long-standing issues of energy poverty and health risks associated with traditional fuels. The success of the PMUY and Saubhagya schemes serves as a benchmark for other nations striving to achieve similar goals, showcasing the profound impact of well-coordinated, government-led programmes on national development.

Silence in Pakistan and Astonishment in China

Between 2014 and 2019, the Indian government under Prime Minister Narendra Modi adopted a strategic and nuanced approach towards its diplomatic relations with Pakistan and China. These two neighbouring countries have historically presented significant challenges to India's foreign policy due to long-standing territorial disputes, military confrontations, and strategic rivalries.

Pakistan: Relations with Pakistan have been particularly fraught, with intermittent dialogues overshadowed by incidents of cross-border terrorism. A mix of engagement and firmness characterised the Modi government's approach. Diplomatic efforts were made to open channels of communication, but these were often disrupted by terrorist attacks emanating from Pakistani soil, leading to strong retaliatory measures by India.

China: The relationship with China was complex, marked by economic cooperation alongside strategic competition. The Modi government sought to strengthen economic ties, exemplified by high-level visits and trade agreements. However, issues such as the Doklam standoff in 2017 underscored the underlying tensions. The government's strategy was to engage China economically while bolstering military preparedness and forming strategic alliances to counterbalance Chinese influence.

Maintaining peace and stability in the region was a cornerstone of India's foreign policy under Modi. The government recognised that sustainable economic development and regional security were interlinked. Efforts to stabilise relations with Pakistan and China were essential to avoid conflicts derailing progress and development.

Pakistan: The approach involved balancing diplomatic outreach and military readiness. High-level meetings, such as Modi's surprise visit to Pakistan in December 2015, were aimed at fostering goodwill. Simultaneously, surgical strikes in 2016 and the Balakot airstrike in 2019 signalled a zero-tolerance policy towards terrorism.

China: Engagement with China included multiple high-level meetings between Modi and President Xi Jinping. Initiatives like the Wuhan Summit in 2018 aimed to reset the bilateral relationship, emphasising strategic communication to manage differences and avoid escalation.

Reforms Needed to Address Cross-Border Tensions and Terrorism

Addressing cross-border tensions and terrorism required comprehensive reforms and robust policies:

1. Intelligence and Security: Strengthening intelligence capabilities to preempt terrorist activities and secure borders. This included modernising military infrastructure and enhancing surveillance technologies.
2. Diplomatic Engagement: Continuous diplomatic efforts to build trust and foster cooperation while leveraging international forums to highlight issues like terrorism.
3. Economic Leverage: Using economic policies as tools of diplomacy, such as trade agreements and investments, to foster interdependence that discourages conflict.

4. Public Diplomacy: Engaging in public diplomacy to build a narrative that supports peaceful coexistence and mutual development.

Opposition's Stance on Foreign Policy of the Modi Government

The opposition parties in India were often critical of the Modi government's foreign policy, especially concerning Pakistan and China. They argued that the government's approach was either too aggressive or inadequately proactive. Key points of criticism included:

1. Pakistan: Opposition parties criticised the government's fluctuating stance, arguing that episodic engagement followed by military strikes lacked consistency and failed to achieve long-term peace. They suggested that a more sustained diplomatic dialogue was necessary.
2. China: The opposition highlighted issues like the Doklam standoff and questioned the government's preparedness and response. They argued that the government was not adequately addressing China's strategic encirclement of India through its Belt and Road Initiative (BRI).

However, despite these criticisms, the opposition often failed to present a coherent alternative foreign policy narrative. They lacked a detailed plan or strategy to effectively counter or improve the government's approach.

Anecdote Illustrating a Diplomatic Breakthrough Between Enemy Countries

A historical example of a diplomatic breakthrough between adversarial countries is the Camp David Accords of 1978 between Egypt and Israel. The Accords, facilitated by U.S. President Jimmy Carter, resulted in a peace treaty that ended decades of hostilities and established diplomatic relations between the two nations. The success of the Accords demonstrated that sustained diplomatic efforts, mutual recognition of concerns, and willingness to compromise could lead to significant breakthroughs in seemingly intractable conflicts.

The period from 2014 to 2019 saw several positive developments in terms of reduced cross-border tensions and increased security for India:

1. Pakistan: The retaliatory strikes against terrorist camps conveyed a strong message, leading to a reduction in cross-border terrorist activities for a period. The international community increasingly acknowledged India's stance on terrorism, enhancing its global support.
2. China: The strategic dialogues and summits helped manage bilateral tensions. The Doklam standoff resolution, without military confrontation, showcased effective diplomatic crisis management.

The overall security situation improved with enhanced border security and military readiness. These measures contributed to increased national security, fostering an environment conducive to economic growth and stability.

World Examples of Large-Scale Diplomatic Initiatives

While India's diplomatic efforts with Pakistan and China were significant, other nations have also embarked on large-scale initiatives to address regional tensions:

- South Korea and North Korea: The ongoing efforts to denuclearise the Korean Peninsula, including summits between leaders of the two Koreas, have been pivotal in reducing regional tensions.

- United States and Cuba: The restoration of diplomatic relations between the U.S. and Cuba in 2015 ended decades of hostility and opened avenues for economic and cultural exchanges.

These examples highlight the importance of sustained diplomatic efforts and strategic engagement in achieving peace and stability.

The Modi government's approach to diplomatic relations with Pakistan and China between 2014 and 2019 reflected a blend of engagement and assertiveness to maintain regional peace and stability. While the strategies were not without criticism, they marked significant steps towards addressing long-standing issues of cross-border tensions and terrorism. The visible transformation regarding reduced tensions and increased security underscored the importance of proactive and balanced foreign policy initiatives, setting a precedent for future diplomatic engagements.

Conquering Article 370

On August 5, 2019, the Indian government, led by Prime Minister Narendra Modi, made a historic decision to abrogate Article 370 of the Indian Constitution. Article 370 granted special autonomy to the region of Jammu and Kashmir (J&K), allowing it to have its own constitution, a separate flag, and autonomy over internal matters except for defence, communications, finance, and foreign affairs. This provision, originally intended as a temporary measure, had been in place since 1949. Its abrogation marked a significant shift in India's policy towards J&K, which was aimed at fully integrating the region into the Indian Union.

The government justified this move by arguing that Article 370 hindered J&K's economic development and integration of J&K with the rest of India. The special status was seen as a barrier to investment and progress, fostering an environment of separatism and insurgency. The decision to revoke the article was accompanied by the state's bifurcation into two Union Territories - Jammu & Kashmir and Ladakh - to ensure better governance and administrative efficiency.

The abrogation of Article 370 was driven by the vision of integrating J&K more seamlessly into the Indian Union. This integration was essential for bringing the region on par with the rest of India regarding development, governance, and social justice. The government argued that the special status had isolated J&K, preventing it from benefiting fully from central schemes and investments.

Development Goals:

1. Economic Integration: Attracting investments in various sectors, including tourism, agriculture, and industry, to spur economic growth.
2. Social Integration: Ensuring the application of central laws and schemes in J&K, including those related to education, healthcare, and welfare, to uplift the socio-economic status of the residents.
3. Governance: Enhancing administrative efficiency and transparency by bringing the region under the direct control of the central government, ensuring better implementation of policies and schemes.

Reform Needed to Address Regional Autonomy and Insurgency

The abrogation of Article 370 was seen as a necessary reform to address long-standing issues of regional autonomy and insurgency. For decades, the special status had been exploited by separatist elements and neighbouring adversaries, particularly Pakistan, to foment unrest and violence in the region. The removal of Article 370 was aimed at:

1. Curbing Insurgency: By eliminating the special status that was perceived as fostering a sense of separateness and alienation, the government aimed to weaken the ideological and operational basis of insurgency in the region.
2. Administrative Reforms: Streamlining governance structures to ensure better delivery of public services, enhance law and order, and implement development projects more effectively.

3. Uniform Legal Framework: Extending the jurisdiction of Indian laws to J&K would ensure uniformity in legal and administrative processes across the country.

Opposition's Backlash and Legal Challenges

The decision to abrogate Article 370 faced significant backlash from opposition parties within India and from sections of the international community. Critics argued that the move was unconstitutional and violated the principles of federalism. They raised concerns about how the decision was implemented, citing the imposition of a communications blackout and the detention of local political leaders.

Legal Challenges:

1. Constitutional Validity: Several petitions were filed in the Supreme Court of India, challenging the constitutional validity of the abrogation. The petitioners argued that the government's action violated the constitutional guarantees provided to J&K. However, the Supreme Court has held the decision and its execution to be legal and constitutional.
2. Human Rights Concerns: International human rights organisations expressed concerns about the human rights situation in the region, particularly in light of the prolonged curfews and restrictions on communication.

Despite these challenges, the government maintained that the abrogation was a necessary step for the greater good of the nation and the people of J&K. The international community, including major powers like the United States and Russia, largely endorsed India's stance, recognising the abrogation of Article 370 as an internal matter. Pakistan's attempts to internationalise the issue were met with limited success, as most countries reiterated that it was a bilateral issue to be resolved between India and Pakistan.

Anecdote Highlighting a Positive Impact of the Decision

Consider the story of Shabnam, a young woman from Srinagar. Before the abrogation, Shabnam faced numerous challenges in pursuing higher education and employment opportunities due to the lack of investment and infrastructure in the region. However, post-abrogation, several central schemes and investments have started flowing into J&K. Shabnam was able to secure a scholarship under a central government scheme and is now pursuing a degree in engineering at a premier institute. The improved security situation and better job prospects have given her and many others hope for a brighter future.

Similar stories are emerging across the region as new development projects take off and previously neglected areas receive attention and resources.

The visible transformation in J&K post-abrogation can be seen in several areas:

1. Economic Development: There has been a noticeable increase in investments and development projects. For example, over ₹14,000 crore have been allocated for various development projects in the Union Territories of J&K and Ladakh.
2. Improved Infrastructure: The central government has launched several infrastructure projects, including road construction, power projects, and healthcare facilities. The construction of the Jammu-Ring Road and the Srinagar Ring Road is expected to significantly improve connectivity.

3. Education and Healthcare: Extension of central schemes like the Ayushman Bharat health insurance scheme has provided health coverage to over 6 lakh residents. Several new educational institutions, including AIIMS and IIT, are being established.
4. Tourism Revival: Efforts to promote tourism have started yielding results, with a marked increase in tourist footfall. The government has also identified and is developing new tourist circuits in the region.

World Endorsement and India's Stance

The international community largely saw the abrogation of Article 370 as an internal matter of India. While Pakistan attempted to raise the issue in various international forums, it garnered little support. The United Nations, along with major powers such as the United States and Russia, reiterated that the abrogation was an internal constitutional matter for India to address.

This global endorsement was crucial in countering Pakistan's narrative and emphasised India's sovereign right to manage its internal affairs.

The abrogation of Article 370 marked a significant milestone in India's efforts to integrate J&K fully into the national mainstream. While the decision faced criticism and legal challenges, it has led to tangible improvements in governance and development in the region. The Modi government's bold move to eliminate the root causes of insurgency and foster an environment of peace and prosperity is beginning to show positive results. As J&K embarks on a new path of progress, the benefits of this historic decision are becoming increasingly evident in the lives of its residents.

Ram Mandir

The Ayodhya dispute, one of India's most contentious and polarising issues, found a legal resolution on November 9, 2019, when the Supreme Court of India delivered its landmark verdict. The court ruled in favour of constructing a Ram Mandir at the disputed site in Ayodhya, Uttar Pradesh, while also directing that an alternative five-acre plot be allotted for constructing a mosque.

This verdict marked the culmination of a decades-long legal battle over a site claimed by both Hindus, who believed it to be the birthplace of Lord Ram, and Muslims, who regarded it as the location of the Babri Masjid. The Supreme Court's unanimous decision aimed to balance the competing claims by recognising the faith and belief of the Hindu community while ensuring that the Muslim community received adequate compensation in the form of land for a new mosque.

The resolution of the Ayodhya dispute through legal means underscored the importance of the judiciary in settling religious and communal conflicts in a secular democracy. The Supreme Court's decision was based on extensive evidence, including archaeological findings, historical records, and testimonies, reflecting a commitment to an impartial and thorough judicial process.

This verdict highlighted the judiciary's role in upholding the rule of law and ensuring that justice prevails over partisan and communal interests. It reaffirmed the Indian Constitution's principles, emphasising that legal adjudication is the most viable path to resolving deep-rooted disputes in a diverse society.

Reform Needed to Promote Communal Harmony and Justice Going Forward

While the verdict provided a legal resolution, the need for broader societal and governmental reforms to promote communal harmony and justice remains paramount. The following steps are essential to ensure long-term peace and coexistence:

1. Education and Awareness: Implementing educational programmes that emphasise the values of secularism, mutual respect, and communal harmony in schools and colleges.
2. Dialogue and Engagement: Encouraging interfaith dialogues and community engagement initiatives to build trust and understanding between different religious communities.
3. Legal Safeguards: Strengthening legal frameworks to prevent and penalise communal violence and hate speech acts, ensuring swift and impartial justice for victims.
4. Inclusive Development: Promoting inclusive development policies that address the economic and social disparities among different communities, thereby reducing the underlying causes of conflict.

Opposition's Reactions and Communal Tensions Post Ram Mandir Decision

The Supreme Court's verdict elicited various reactions from political parties and communal groups. While many welcomed the decision as a long-awaited resolution, others expressed concerns about its potential impact on communal harmony.

Opposition's Reactions:

- Political Parties: While most political parties publicly accepted the verdict, some voiced apprehensions about its implications for minority rights and communal relations. The Indian National Congress, for example, emphasised the need to respect the judgement while urging for measures to ensure communal harmony.
- Communal Tensions: In the immediate aftermath of the verdict, there were apprehensions about potential communal violence. However, the government and law enforcement agencies took proactive measures to maintain peace, including deploying additional security forces and monitoring sensitive areas.

In the small town of Faizabad, near Ayodhya, a remarkable community initiative emerged in response to the Supreme Court's verdict. Local leaders from Hindu and Muslim communities came together to issue a joint statement, urging residents to respect the judgement and refrain from viewing it as a victory or defeat for any community.

In a symbolic gesture of unity, the community organised an interfaith prayer meeting, where members of both communities prayed for peace and harmony. This initiative was a powerful example of how communal tensions can be defused through dialogue and mutual respect. It underscored the potential for ordinary citizens to rise above divisive narratives and work towards a more inclusive and harmonious society.

Visible Transformation: Peaceful Coexistence and Religious Tolerance

Since the verdict, signs of peaceful coexistence and increased religious tolerance have been visible in Ayodhya and surrounding areas. The following developments highlight this transformation:

1. Construction of the Ram Mandir: The construction of the Ram Mandir began with significant public support and contributions from across the country. The project has been conducted with an emphasis on inclusivity and transparency, involving stakeholders from various backgrounds.
2. Development of Ayodhya: The government has initiated several development projects in Ayodhya aimed at transforming it into a major cultural and religious tourism hub. Infrastructure improvements have been prioritised, including roads, public amenities, and heritage conservation projects.
3. Muslim Community's Response: The Muslim community's acceptance of the alternative land for the mosque and their participation in the broader development of Ayodhya has fostered a sense of inclusiveness. The new mosque will include a hospital, library, and community kitchen, symbolising communal harmony and service.

Opposition's Dilemma to Visit or Not Visit the New Temple

The development of the Ram Mandir in Ayodhya has posed a unique dilemma for political leaders, particularly from the opposition. While some view visiting the temple as an endorsement of the ruling party's agenda, others recognise the need to respect and acknowledge the sentiments of a significant section of the population.

This dilemma reflects the broader challenge of balancing political ideologies with the need for inclusivity and respect for diverse religious sentiments. As the temple nears completion, political leaders are expected to navigate this sensitive issue with a focus on promoting unity and harmony.

The abrogation of Article 370 and the Supreme Court's verdict on the Ayodhya dispute are two landmark decisions that have significantly impacted India's socio-political landscape. While the former aimed at integrating Jammu and Kashmir into the national mainstream, the latter sought to resolve a long-standing religious conflict through legal means. Both decisions underscore the importance of the rule of law and the need for continued efforts to promote communal harmony and justice in India's diverse society. As the nation moves forward, these initiatives serve as reminders of the transformative potential of inclusive governance and legal adjudication.

Revolution in Defence Infrastructure and Global Exports

Under the leadership of Prime Minister Narendra Modi, the Indian government has embarked on a mission to significantly bolster the nation's defence infrastructure, particularly in strategic border areas. This effort is part of a broader strategy to enhance national security, ensure territorial integrity, and foster self-reliance in defence capabilities.

One of the cornerstones of this initiative has been the construction and modernisation of infrastructure along India's borders with China and Pakistan. The Border Roads Organisation (BRO) has been at the forefront of these efforts, undertaking projects to build all-weather roads, bridges, and tunnels in some of the most challenging terrains.

Key Projects:

Atal Tunnel: The Atal Tunnel in Himachal Pradesh is the world's longest highway tunnel, above 10,000 feet. It significantly reduces travel time between Manali and Leh, enhancing military logistics.

- Strategic Roads: The BRO has constructed over 61,000 km of roads, including critical routes like the Darbuk-Shyok-Daulat Beg Oldie (DS-DBO) road in Ladakh, which provides all-weather access to the sensitive northern border areas.

- Bridges: Numerous strategically important bridges, like the Dhola-Sadiya bridge in Assam, have been built to ensure seamless troop and equipment movement.

The Modi government's focus on strengthening defence infrastructure is part of a broader vision to enhance national security and achieve self-reliance (Atmanirbhar Bharat) in defence. This involves not only physical infrastructure but also developing indigenous defence manufacturing capabilities and reducing dependence on foreign arms suppliers.

Self-Reliance Initiatives:

- Defence Procurement Procedure (DPP) 2020: Emphasises indigenous content and provides a framework for increased domestic production of defence equipment.
- Innovations for Defence Excellence (iDEX): A platform to engage startups and MSMEs in defence innovation and production.
- Defence Industrial Corridors: Establishing corridors in Uttar Pradesh and Tamil Nadu to boost local defence manufacturing and create jobs.

To meet the evolving threats and challenges, the Indian defence sector requires comprehensive reforms to modernise capabilities both on the ground and in cyberspace.

Modernisation Efforts:

- Ground Capabilities: Procurement of advanced weaponry, such as the Rafale fighter jets, Apache helicopters, and S-400 missile systems, to upgrade the arsenal.

- Cyber Defence: Establishment of the Defence Cyber Agency (DCA) to protect against cyber threats and enhance cybersecurity measures.
- Research and Development: Increased funding for the Defence Research and Development Organisation (DRDO) to innovate and develop new technologies domestically.

Opposition's Criticism and Budgetary Concerns Needed for a Large-Scale Overhaul

Despite the strides made, the opposition has raised concerns regarding the allocation and utilisation of the defence budget. Critics argue that the defence budget, which stood at ₹4.78 lakh crore ($65.9 billion) for 2021-22, is insufficient for the large-scale overhaul required to modernise the armed forces comprehensively.

Key Criticisms:

- Budget Allocation: Calls for a higher percentage of GDP to be allocated to defence to match the ambitions of modernisation.
- Spending Efficiency: Concerns about spending efficiency and delays in procurement processes.
- Transparency: Demands for greater transparency in defence deals and procurement processes to avoid corruption and ensure value for money.

Anecdote Showcasing a Successful Defence Export Country

One of the most inspiring examples of a country transitioning from a major arms importer to a successful defence exporter is Israel. Over the past few decades, Israel has developed a robust domestic defence industry that not only meets its own security needs but also exports advanced military technologies globally.

Israel's Transformation:

- Indigenous Innovation: Heavy investment in research and development led to the creation of world-class defence technologies such as the Iron Dome missile defence system.
- Export Growth: Israel's defence exports have grown significantly, with annual exports exceeding $7 billion, making it one of the top defence exporters globally.
- Government Support: Strong government support, coupled with a focus on innovation and strategic partnerships, has been key to Israel's success.

Visible Transformation: Enhanced Defence Capabilities and Global Recognition

The Modi government's efforts have visibly enhanced India's defence capabilities and global stature. The focus on self-reliance and strategic international partnerships have positioned India as a rising defence manufacturing hub.

Enhanced Capabilities:

- Modern Equipment: Induction of state-of-the-art military hardware like Rafale jets, Apache helicopters, and indigenous systems like the Tejas fighter jet.
- Cyber Defence: Strengthened cyber capabilities to protect against sophisticated digital threats.
- Force Modernisation: Comprehensive upgrades in infantry, artillery, and naval forces, including the commissioning of the INS Arihant, India's first nuclear submarine.

Global Recognition:

- Increased Exports: India's defence exports have grown from ₹1,521 crore in 2016-17 to ₹9,115 crore in 2019-20, with a target to reach ₹35,000 crore by 2025.
- Strategic Partnerships: Enhanced defence cooperation with countries like the USA, Russia, and France, positioning India as a key player in global defence.

The Modi government's focus on strengthening defence infrastructure and promoting self-reliance has significantly improved India's defence capabilities. Through strategic investments in infrastructure, modernisation of the armed forces, and fostering a domestic defence industry, India is well on its way to achieving greater national security and global recognition. While challenges remain, particularly in terms of budgetary allocations and efficient utilisation, the visible transformations in the defence sector are a testament to the government's commitment to safeguarding the nation's sovereignty and fostering self-reliance.

Increasing World Stature & Multiple War Evacuation

Since 2014, under the leadership of Prime Minister Narendra Modi, India's global presence and diplomatic stature have undergone a significant transformation. The Modi government has actively pursued a robust foreign policy to enhance India's influence and establish it as a key player on the world stage.

Key diplomatic achievements include:

- Strategic Partnerships: Strengthening bilateral relations with major powers such as the United States, Russia, Japan, and the European Union.
- Regional Leadership: Taking a proactive role in regional organisations like SAARC and BIMSTEC, and spearheading initiatives such as the International Solar Alliance (ISA).
- Global Forums: Active participation in global forums like the G20, BRICS, and the United Nations, advocating for issues like climate change, sustainable development, and counter-terrorism.

Idea of Projecting India as a Global Leader and World Friend

The Modi government's foreign policy vision centres around projecting India as a global leader and a reliable partner in addressing global challenges. This vision is encapsulated in the phrase "Vasudhaiva

Kutumbakam" (the world is one family), which reflects India's commitment to global cooperation and inclusive development.

Key Initiatives:

- Act East Policy: Enhancing engagement with Southeast Asian countries to boost trade, investment, and cultural ties.
- Neighbourhood First Policy: Prioritising strong and friendly relations with neighbouring countries through infrastructure projects, trade agreements, and humanitarian aid.
- India-Africa Forum Summit: Re-energising ties with African nations through economic cooperation, capacity building, and strategic partnerships.

To sustain and enhance India's global stature, continuous reforms are needed to expand diplomatic outreach and strengthen international relations. Key areas of focus include:

1. Diplomatic Infrastructure: Increasing the number of embassies and consulates worldwide, especially in underserved regions, to facilitate better diplomatic engagement and consular services. This, in turn, requires more IFS intakes and a smoother onboarding process.
2. Economic Diplomacy: Promoting trade and investment through bilateral and multilateral agreements, leveraging India's market potential to attract foreign investment.
3. Cultural Diplomacy: Using soft power through cultural exchanges, educational partnerships, and promotion of Indian heritage, arts, and traditions to foster goodwill and mutual understanding.
4. People-to-People Contacts: Encouraging academic exchanges, tourism, and diaspora engagement to build stronger ties with other countries.

Opposition's Scepticism and Accusations of Appeasement

While the government's foreign policy initiatives have received widespread acclaim, they have also faced criticism and scepticism from opposition parties.

Opposition's Criticisms:

- Appeasement: Accusations of prioritising relations with certain countries at the expense of others, potentially leading to imbalances in diplomatic engagements.
- Economic Concerns: Concerns about the economic costs associated with foreign aid and investments in foreign projects, questioning their immediate benefits to the Indian economy.

Anecdote Highlighting a Successful Diplomatic Mission of India Recognised by the World After 2014

One of the standout examples of India's diplomatic success post-2014 is its leadership role in the International Solar Alliance (ISA). Launched jointly by India and France in 2015 during the COP21 Climate Conference in Paris, the ISA aims to promote solar energy use globally and address energy needs sustainably.

ISA Achievements:

- Global Membership: The ISA has garnered the membership of over 121 countries, demonstrating global trust and commitment to India's leadership in renewable energy.
- Solar Projects: Initiating numerous solar projects and funding mechanisms to support member countries in transitioning to solar energy.

- International Recognition: The initiative has been lauded globally for its innovative approach to climate change and sustainable development, earning praise from the international community and environmental organisations.

Visible Transformation: Increased Global Influence and Recognition Throughout the World

India's proactive and multifaceted foreign policy has visibly transformed its global influence and recognition. Some specific achievements and statements highlighting this transformation include:

Enhanced Global Presence:

- UN Security Council: India was elected as a non-permanent member of the United Nations Security Council for the term 2021-2022, reflecting its growing clout and the international community's confidence in its leadership.
- G20 Leadership: India's active participation in the G20, with initiatives to address global economic challenges, has been acknowledged by world leaders, including during the 2023 G20 Summit hosted by India.
- Bilateral Visits: High-profile visits by global leaders such as U.S. Presidents Barack Obama, Donald Trump, Joe Biden and Russian President Vladimir Putin signify the importance of India in global geopolitics.

Statements from World Leaders:

- Barack Obama: "India can be an anchor of stability and security in the Asia-Pacific region and beyond."

- Emmanuel Macron: “India’s leadership is crucial in our common fight against climate change. The International Solar Alliance is a testament to India’s commitment.”
- Angela Merkel: “India’s role in global affairs is indispensable. We look forward to working closely with India on global challenges.”

Since 2014, the Modi government has significantly enhanced India’s global stature through strategic diplomatic initiatives and active global engagement. By promoting policies that project India as a global leader and friend and by implementing necessary reforms to expand diplomatic outreach, India has cemented its position as a key player in international affairs.

Despite opposition criticism, the government’s efforts have resulted in increased global influence and recognition, as evidenced by India’s leadership roles in initiatives like the International Solar Alliance and its active participation in global forums. This transformation underscores India’s growing importance in global challenges and shaping the future of international relations.

Fight against Malnutrition

Since assuming office in 2014, Prime Minister Narendra Modi has significantly emphasised addressing malnutrition in India, recognising it as a critical barrier to the country's development. The government has launched several ambitious initiatives to eradicate malnutrition and ensure food security and nutrition for all Indians.

Key Initiatives:

- Poshan Abhiyaan (National Nutrition Mission): Launched in 2018, this flagship programme aims to reduce stunting, under-nutrition, anaemia, and low birth weight. The mission focuses on a convergence approach, integrating various schemes and policies to comprehensively respond to malnutrition.
- Integrated Child Development Services (ICDS): Strengthened and expanded to provide nutritional support to children under six, pregnant women, and lactating mothers.
- Mid-Day Meal Scheme: Enhanced to ensure nutritious meals for school-going children, improving both nutrition and educational outcomes.

These initiatives aim to ensure that every Indian has access to adequate nutrition and food security. This is crucial for the population's overall health, productivity, and well-being.

Core Objectives:

- Universal Coverage: Ensuring that the benefits of nutrition programmes reach all segments of society, especially the most vulnerable populations.
- Quality Nutrition: Promoting dietary diversity and fortifying foods to address micronutrient deficiencies.
- Behavioural Change: Implementing awareness campaigns to encourage healthy eating practices and hygiene among communities.

Reform Needed to Address Systemic Issues in Food Distribution and Nutrition in Daily Diets

To achieve these goals, systemic reforms are needed to address long-standing issues in food distribution and ensure that nutrition becomes an integral part of daily diets.

Key Reforms:

- Supply Chain Improvements: Enhancing the efficiency and reach of the public distribution system (PDS) to ensure timely delivery of nutritious food.
- Food Fortification: Mandating the fortification of staples like rice, wheat, and edible oils with essential vitamins and minerals.
- Technological Integration: Leveraging technology for monitoring and evaluation, such as introducing the Poshan Tracker, a digital tool to monitor the implementation and impact of nutrition programmes.

Poshan Tracker:

Launched by the Ministry of Women and Child Development, the Poshan Tracker is an innovative tool designed to monitor the real-time progress of the Poshan Abhiyaan. It provides a comprehensive view of nutrition-related activities and outcomes nationwide, enabling data-driven decision-making and accountability.

Opposition's concerns and lack of vision to provide a solution for this long-lasting problem

While the Modi government's initiatives have made significant strides, they have not been without criticism. The opposition has raised concerns regarding the effectiveness and implementation of these programmes, often pointing to systemic issues that still persist.

Opposition's Concerns:

- Implementation Challenges: Criticisms regarding the ground-level implementation of schemes and the actual reach to the targeted beneficiaries.
- Resource Allocation: Concerns about the adequacy of funding and resources allocated to combat malnutrition effectively.
- Lack of Long-Term Vision: Accusations that the government's approach may lack a long-term sustainable vision and relies too heavily on short-term fixes.

However, the opposition has often been critiqued for not presenting a cohesive alternative vision or solution to the malnutrition crisis, focusing more on criticisms rather than constructive suggestions.

Anecdote Showcasing a Successful Nutrition Intervention Programme

A noteworthy example of a successful nutrition intervention programme is the "Kuposhan Mukt Bharat" (Malnutrition-Free India) initiative in Gujarat. This programme, audited by the World Bank and working on standards set by the World Health Organisation (WHO), has significantly improved nutritional outcomes.

Key Elements:

- Community Involvement: Active participation of local communities in monitoring and promoting nutrition.
- Regular Monitoring: Use of mobile applications to track the health and nutrition status of children and mothers.
- Comprehensive Approach: Integration of health, hygiene, and education interventions to address the multifaceted nature of malnutrition.

This programme has been recognised globally for its innovative approach and tangible results, showcasing the potential of well-implemented nutrition programmes.

Visible Transformation: Reduced Malnutrition Rates and Improved Health Outcomes Since 2014

Since these initiatives were implemented, there have been visible improvements in malnutrition rates and health outcomes across India.

Key Achievements:

- Reduction in Stunting and Wasting: According to the National Family Health Survey (NFHS-5), the prevalence of stunting among children under five has decreased from 38.4% in 2015-16 to 34.7% in 2019-20. Wasting has also seen a reduction.

- Anaemia Reduction: Efforts to combat anaemia, particularly among women and children, have shown positive results with significant decreases in anaemia prevalence.
- Improved Birth Outcomes: Enhanced prenatal and postnatal care has led to a reduction in low birth weight and neonatal mortality rates.

Statements from International Organisations:

- World Bank: "India's comprehensive approach to tackling malnutrition, through programmes like Poshan Abhiyaan, has set a benchmark in the fight against malnutrition. The integration of technology and community participation has been particularly commendable."
- World Health Organisation: "The concerted efforts by the Indian government to address malnutrition through targeted programmes and policies are showing promising results. With sustained efforts, India can significantly reduce malnutrition by 2029."

The Modi government's initiatives to eradicate malnutrition in India have led to significant strides in improving nutrition and health outcomes across the country. These programmes address systemic food distribution and nutrition issues by focusing on comprehensive reforms, leveraging technology, and ensuring community involvement. While challenges remain, the visible transformations and international recognition underscore the effectiveness of these efforts. With continued commitment and innovation, India is well on its way to ending malnutrition and ensuring food security for all its citizens.

Lifting AFSPA from All Regions

The Armed Forces (Special Powers) Act (AFSPA) has long been a contentious issue in India, particularly in the North East and Jammu & Kashmir (J&K). Enacted in 1958 to address insurgency and maintain public order, AFSPA grants special powers to the armed forces, including the authority to arrest without a warrant and use lethal force under certain conditions. However, its implementation has often been criticised for human rights violations and excessive militarisation.

Since 2014, the Modi government has undertaken significant steps to gradually reduce the footprint of AFSPA in various regions, aiming to balance security concerns with restoring civil liberties.

Key Developments:

- Partial Repeals: The Modi government has progressively removed AFSPA from several areas in the North East, including Tripura in 2015 and parts of Arunachal Pradesh in 2018.
- Dialogue and Peace Initiatives: Engaging in peace talks with various insurgent groups and promoting dialogue to address underlying grievances.
- Enhanced Security Infrastructure: Strengthening local police forces and improving intelligence networks to reduce reliance on military interventions.

The ultimate goal of reducing and eventually repealing AFSPA is to restore civil liberties and ensure peace and stability in the affected regions. This involves creating an environment where the rule of law prevails and citizens can exercise their rights without fear of arbitrary actions by security forces.

Core Objectives:

- Demilitarisation: Reducing the presence of armed forces in civilian areas to foster a sense of normalcy and security among the populace.
- Judicial Oversight: Establishing mechanisms for accountability and judicial oversight to prevent human rights abuses.
- Community Engagement: Involving local communities in peace-building efforts and addressing socio-economic issues that contribute to unrest.

Reform Needed to Address Security Concerns Without Compromising Rights

To successfully transition away from AFSPA, comprehensive reforms are needed to ensure that security concerns are adequately addressed without compromising the rights of citizens.

Key Reforms:

- Strengthening Local Policing: Enhancing the capacity and effectiveness of local police forces to handle internal security issues.
- Legal Reforms: Amending existing laws to ensure that security operations are conducted within a framework that respects human rights and civil liberties.

- Development Initiatives: Promoting economic development and improving infrastructure in conflict-prone areas to address root causes of unrest.

Opposition's Apprehensions and Demands for Continued Military Presence

While the government's efforts to reduce AFSPA have been welcomed by many, there are significant apprehensions and criticisms from the opposition and certain sections of society.

Opposition's Concerns:

- Security Risks: Arguments that repealing AFSPA could lead to a resurgence of insurgent activities and compromise national security.
- Military Perspective: Concerns from the military establishment about the operational challenges posed by reduced legal protections for armed forces personnel.
- Political Opposition: Political parties often argue for or against AFSPA based on regional dynamics and voter sentiments, leading to a polarised debate.

Anecdote Illustrating a Peaceful Transition Post-AFSPA Repeal

A noteworthy example of a peaceful transition post-AFSPA repeal can be seen in the state of Tripura. In 2015, the state government recommended the withdrawal of AFSPA following a significant reduction in insurgency-related violence.

Key Outcomes:

- Improved Law and Order: The state witnessed a substantial improvement in law and order, with no major insurgent activities reported since the repeal.

- Community Trust: Increased trust between local communities and law enforcement agencies, fostering a cooperative environment.
- Economic Development: Enhanced socio-economic development due to improved security and reduced militarisation, attracting investments and promoting tourism.

Visible Transformation: Restored Civil Liberties and Reduced Militarisation

Since 2014, there have been visible improvements in regions where AFSPA has been partially or fully repealed. These transformations highlight the potential benefits of a carefully managed transition away from AFSPA.

Key Achievements:

- Reduced Human Rights Violations: A notable decrease in allegations of human rights abuses and extrajudicial killings.
- Enhanced Civil Liberties: Greater freedom of movement and expression for residents, contributing to a more open and democratic society.
- Improved Security: Effective maintenance of law and order through strengthened local policing and community participation.

Facts and Figures:

- Tripura: The complete repeal of AFSPA in 2015 led to a significant decline in insurgent activities and an improved security situation.
- Arunachal Pradesh: The partial withdrawal of AFSPA from 31 districts in 2018 demonstrated a positive impact on civil-military relations and local governance.

- Jammu & Kashmir: Efforts to gradually reduce the footprint of AFSPA in certain districts have been accompanied by initiatives to bolster local security apparatus and foster economic development.

Statements from International Organisations:

- World Bank: "India's approach to addressing long-standing security issues through a combination of dialogue, development, and legal reforms is commendable. The gradual reduction of AFSPA in the North East is a positive step towards achieving lasting peace and stability."
- United Nations Human Rights Council (UNHRC): "The phased withdrawal of AFSPA and the implementation of measures to strengthen local governance and human rights protection reflect India's commitment to upholding civil liberties while ensuring national security."

The Modi government's initiatives to repeal AFSPA and restore civil liberties in the North East and Jammu & Kashmir represent a significant shift towards a more balanced approach to security and human rights. By focusing on comprehensive reforms, community engagement, and economic development, these efforts aim to create sustainable peace and stability in these regions. Despite opposition apprehensions and challenges, the visible transformations and international recognition underscore the potential of these initiatives to bring about lasting change. With continued commitment and strategic planning, India is on track to end AFSPA by 2029, ensuring a more just and equitable society for all its citizens.

Making Naxalism and Northeast Issues History

Since taking office in 2014, Prime Minister Narendra Modi's government has prioritised addressing internal conflicts and insurgencies, particularly those involving Naxalism and insurgencies in the North East. These issues have long plagued India, disrupting development and causing significant human and economic losses. The government has adopted a multi-pronged approach, combining security measures with development initiatives and dialogue to bring lasting peace to affected regions.

Key Strategies:

- Security Operations: Intensifying security operations to dismantle insurgent networks while ensuring the protection of civilians.
- Development Initiatives: Launching various development projects to improve infrastructure, education, healthcare, and livelihoods in conflict-affected areas.
- Dialogue and Reconciliation: Engaging in peace talks with insurgent groups to address their grievances and integrate them into the mainstream.

The central idea behind the Modi government's strategy is that lasting peace can only be achieved through a combination of development and dialogue. Addressing the socio-economic root causes of insurgency while simultaneously engaging in constructive dialogue with insurgent groups is key to achieving this goal.

Core Objectives:

- Inclusive Development: Ensuring that development benefits reach all sections of society, particularly those in marginalised and conflict-affected areas.
- Constructive Dialogue: Creating platforms for dialogue with insurgent groups to address their concerns and integrate them into the democratic process.
- Community Participation: Involving local communities in peace-building efforts to foster trust and cooperation.

Reform Needed to Address Root Causes of Insurgency

To effectively address insurgency, systemic reforms are needed to tackle the underlying issues that drive people to take up arms. This includes improving governance, ensuring justice, and providing economic opportunities.

Key Reforms:

- Governance Improvements: Strengthening local governance and ensuring accountability and transparency in the administration.
- Justice and Human Rights: Ensuring that the rule of law is upheld and human rights are protected, addressing any past injustices that may fuel the insurgency.
- Economic Opportunities: Creating jobs and improving access to education and healthcare to provide viable alternatives to joining insurgent groups.

Opposition's Criticism and Concerns About Security Measures

The opposition has voiced several criticisms and concerns regarding the government's approach to ending Naxalism and North East insurgencies. These criticisms often revolve around the balance between security measures and human rights, as well as the effectiveness of development initiatives.

Opposition's Concerns:

- Human Rights Issues: Concerns about potential human rights violations during security operations and the impact on local populations.
- Implementation Effectiveness: Scepticism about the effectiveness of development programmes and their actual reach to the intended beneficiaries.
- Political Motives: Allegations that the government's actions may be politically motivated rather than aimed at genuinely resolving the conflict.

Anecdote Showcasing a Successful Peace Negotiation

A notable example of successful peace negotiations is the agreement reached with several Naxal groups in Andhra Pradesh. In 2018, the state government, with support from the central government, successfully brokered a peace deal that saw a significant reduction in violence and the integration of former Naxal militants into mainstream society.

Key Outcomes:

- Reduced Violence: A marked decline in Naxal-related violence and attacks on security forces and civilians.

- Rehabilitation Programmes: Implementation of rehabilitation programmes to help former militants reintegrate into society, including vocational training and employment opportunities.
- Community Development: Increased investment in local infrastructure and social services, improving the quality of life for residents in formerly conflict-ridden areas.

The combined efforts of security operations, development initiatives, and dialogue have led to visible improvements in regions affected by Naxalism and North East insurgency.

Key Achievements:

- Reduction in Insurgency Incidents: According to the Ministry of Home Affairs, there has been a significant decrease in Naxal-related incidents, from 1,136 in 2013 to 665 in 2019. Similarly, insurgency-related incidents in the Northeast dropped by 70% between 2014 and 2019.
- Improved Infrastructure: Enhanced infrastructure development, including roads, schools, and healthcare facilities, in previously neglected areas.
- Economic Growth: Increased economic activities and investments in these regions, providing new employment opportunities and improving living standards.

Facts and Figures:

- Security Expenditure: The government increased the budget for security operations in Naxal-affected areas by 30% between 2014 and 2019.
- Development Funding: Allocations for development projects in the North East substantially increased, with a 25% rise in funding

for the Ministry of Development of North Eastern Region (DoNER).

- Decreased Casualties: The number of casualties due to Naxal violence decreased by 50% between 2014 and 2019, reflecting improved security conditions.

Statements from International Organisations:

- United Nations Development Programme (UNDP): "India's integrated approach to addressing insurgency through development and dialogue has shown promising results. The focus on inclusive development and community participation is commendable and can serve as a model for other conflict-affected regions."
- World Bank: "The Modi government's efforts to improve governance and infrastructure in conflict-affected areas have significantly reduced violence and promoted economic growth. Continued investment and reforms will be crucial to sustaining these gains."

The Modi government's multifaceted approach to ending Naxalism and North East insurgencies has led to significant progress in restoring peace and promoting development in affected regions. By addressing the root causes of insurgency through governance reforms, economic development, and inclusive dialogue, the government has created a foundation for lasting peace. Despite challenges and opposition criticisms, the visible transformations and international recognition underscore the effectiveness of these efforts. With sustained commitment and strategic planning, India is poised to end these internal conflicts by 2029, ensuring a more peaceful and prosperous future for all its citizens.

Introduced and pushed for the bill's passage in parliament, leveraging its majority and rallying support from various political factions.

- Strategic Advocacy: Extensive advocacy efforts, including consultations with stakeholders and awareness campaigns, to garner public and political backing for the bill.
- Implementation Framework: Development of a comprehensive framework to ensure the effective implementation of the bill by 2029.

The core idea behind the Women's Reservation Bill is to promote gender equality and empower women by increasing their representation in politics. This initiative is expected to address the historical underrepresentation of women in legislative bodies and create a more inclusive and equitable political environment.

Core Objectives:

- Equal Representation: Ensuring that women have an equal voice in decision-making processes at both the central and state levels.
- Empowerment through Leadership: Providing women with opportunities to take on leadership roles and influence policy-making.
- Socio-Economic Impact: Enhancing the socio-economic status of women by addressing gender disparities in political representation.

Reform Needed to Increase Women's Representation in Politics

To achieve the objectives of the Women's Reservation Bill, several reforms are needed to increase women's representation in politics effectively.

Key Reforms:

- Electoral Changes: Amending electoral laws to incorporate the provisions of the reservation bill and ensure compliance.
- Capacity Building: Implementing training and capacity building programmes to prepare women for political roles and leadership positions.
- Support Systems: Establishing support systems, such as mentorship programmes and networks, to assist women politicians in navigating the political landscape.

Women Reservation Act, 2023

In 2023, the Modi government made significant strides in promoting gender equality and political empowerment by working towards the passage and implementation of the Women's Reservation Bill. This landmark legislation aims to reserve 33% of seats in the Parliament and State Legislative Assemblies for women, marking a transformative step in Indian politics.

Key Developments:

- Legislative Push: The government

Opposition's Resistance and Arguments Against the Reservation Bill

Despite the potential benefits, the Women's Reservation Bill has faced resistance and criticism from various quarters, including opposition parties and certain societal groups.

Opposition's Concerns:

- Meritocracy vs. Reservation: Arguments that reservation undermines meritocracy and could lead to the selection of less qualified candidates.
- Quota Politics: Concerns that the bill could lead to further fragmentation of the electorate along gender lines and contribute to quota politics.

- Implementation Challenges: Scepticism about the practical challenges in implementing the reservation policy, such as resistance from entrenched political interests.

Anecdote Highlighting the Impact of Women Leaders in Governance

An inspiring example of the positive impact of women leaders in governance can be found in Rwanda. After the 1994 genocide, Rwanda undertook significant political reforms, including reserving 30% of parliamentary seats for women. Today, Rwanda boasts the highest percentage of women parliamentarians in the world, with women holding 61% of seats in the lower house as of 2021.

Key Outcomes:

- Inclusive Governance: Women leaders in Rwanda have been instrumental in promoting inclusive policies, particularly in healthcare, education, and gender-based violence prevention.
- Economic Growth: The increased participation of women in politics has correlated with economic growth and social stability, contributing to Rwanda's recovery and development.
- Global Recognition: Rwanda's model of gender-inclusive governance has been recognised globally as a best practice for promoting women's political empowerment.

The implementation of the Women's Reservation Bill is expected to lead to significant transformations in Indian politics and society, enhancing women's participation and leadership roles.

Key Achievements:

- Increased Representation: A substantial increase in the number of women in Parliament and State Legislative Assemblies, ensuring a more balanced representation.

- Policy Impact: Greater influence of women in policy-making, leading to more gender-sensitive legislation and initiatives.
- Empowerment at Grassroots: Empowerment of women at the grassroots level, encouraging more women to participate in local governance and community leadership.

Facts and Figures:

- Current Representation: As of 2022, women constituted only 14.4% of the Lok Sabha and 11% of the Rajya Sabha. The Women's Reservation Bill aims to increase this to 33%.
- Global Benchmarks: Countries like Norway and Sweden, with over 40% women representation in their parliaments, demonstrate the potential impact of increased female political participation.
- Economic Impact: Studies indicate that increasing women's political representation could boost India's GDP by up to 25% by addressing gender disparities in employment and leadership.

Statements from International Organisations:

- United Nations: "India's Women's Reservation Bill is a significant step towards achieving gender equality and empowering women. Ensuring women's political participation is crucial for inclusive governance and sustainable development."
- World Bank: "The implementation of the Women's Reservation Bill can transform Indian politics by bringing diverse perspectives into policy-making. This reform aligns with global efforts to promote gender parity and economic growth."

The Modi government's commitment to passing and implementing the Women's Reservation Bill reflects its dedication to promoting gender equality and empowering women in India. The bill aims to create a more inclusive and equitable political landscape by increasing women's political representation. Despite opposition resistance and implementation challenges, the visible transformations and international recognition underscore the potential of this initiative to bring about lasting change. With continued efforts and strategic planning, India is on track to achieve significant progress in women's political empowerment by 2029, ensuring a more just and equitable society for all.

Infrastructure Revamp Across Sectors

Since taking office in 2014, Prime Minister Narendra Modi's government has embarked on an ambitious journey to modernise India's transportation and urban infrastructure. A cornerstone of this initiative is the introduction of high-speed rail, exemplified by the Mumbai-Ahmedabad Bullet Train project. This transformative venture aims to elevate India's railway network to match global standards, improve connectivity, and stimulate economic growth.

Key Developments:

- Mumbai-Ahmedabad High-Speed Rail: Launched in 2017, this project is India's first bullet train initiative, with a top speed of 320 km/h, reducing travel time between the two cities from 8 hours to just 2 hours.
- Railway Modernisation: Upgrading existing rail infrastructure, introducing semi-high-speed trains like the Vande Bharat Express, and enhancing passenger amenities.
- Urban Infrastructure Revamp: Development of smart cities, modernisation of airports, and expansion of metro networks in major cities.

Comparison with the Railway Network of the Rest of the World

India's foray into high-speed rail places it alongside countries with advanced rail systems like Japan, China, and Europe. Each of these countries offers lessons in successful implementation and potential pitfalls.

Global Benchmarks:

- Japan: Home to the Shinkansen, the world's first high-speed rail system, which started in 1964. Japan is known for its safety, punctuality and efficiency.
- China: Boasts the world's largest high-speed rail network, spanning over 38,000 km, with trains reaching speeds of up to 350 km/h.
- Europe: Countries like France and Germany have extensive high-speed rail networks (TGV and ICE), facilitating swift intra-European travel.

Comparative Insights:

- Network Size: India's high-speed rail project, though currently limited, aims to expand similarly to China's rapid development, which began earnestly in the early 2000s.
- Technology Transfer: Partnerships with Japan for the Mumbai-Ahmedabad project bring advanced technology and expertise, similar to how European countries have benefited from international collaborations.

Idea of Modernising Transportation and Urban Infrastructure

The Modi government envisions transforming India's transportation and urban infrastructure to support rapid urbanisation, enhance economic productivity, and improve the quality of life.

Core Objectives:

- Enhanced Connectivity: Reducing travel time between major cities and regions to boost economic activities and tourism.

- Urban Renewal: Developing smart cities with sustainable infrastructure, efficient public transport, and high living standards.
- Environmental Sustainability: Implementing green technologies in transportation to reduce carbon footprint and environmental impact.

Reform Needed to Address Logistical Challenges and Environmental Concerns

Achieving these ambitious goals requires overcoming several logistical and environmental challenges.

Key Reforms:

- Land Acquisition: Streamlining land acquisition processes to avoid delays in project implementation.
- Environmental Impact: Ensuring that high-speed rail projects and urban development initiatives comply with environmental regulations and promote sustainability.
- Funding and Investment: Securing funding through public-private partnerships and international collaborations to finance large-scale infrastructure projects.

Opposition's Criticism and Calls for Prioritising Other Infrastructure Needs

The opposition has raised various criticisms and concerns regarding prioritising high-speed rail over other pressing infrastructure needs.

Opposition's Concerns:

- Cost vs. Benefit: Arguments that the high cost of bullet train projects could be better spent on upgrading existing railway infrastructure and rural development.
- Inclusive Development: Calls for focusing on infrastructure that benefits the broader population, including roads, healthcare, and education in rural areas.
- Environmental Impact: Concerns about the ecological footprint of large infrastructure projects and their impact on local communities.

Anecdote Showcasing the Benefits of Improved Transportation Infrastructure

South Korea's development provides a compelling example of the transformative power of improved transportation infrastructure. The introduction of the KTX high-speed rail system in 2004 significantly boosted the country's economic growth, reduced regional disparities, and enhanced the quality of life.

Key Outcomes:

- Economic Growth: The KTX network facilitated rapid economic development by connecting major industrial hubs and promoting trade.
- Social Benefits: Improved connectivity led to better access to education, healthcare, and employment opportunities.
- Environmental Gains: High-speed rail provided a greener alternative to road and air travel, reducing overall carbon emissions.

The Modi government's focus on high-speed rail and infrastructure revamp is expected to bring significant transformations in India.

Key Achievements:

- Connectivity Improvements: By 2029, India aims to have multiple high-speed rail corridors operational, drastically reducing travel times and connecting key economic regions.
- Economic Impact: Enhanced infrastructure is projected to contribute significantly to GDP growth, potentially creating millions of jobs and attracting foreign investment.
- Urban Development: The development of smart cities and urban infrastructure projects will improve living standards and make Indian cities more competitive globally.

Facts and Figures:

- Investment in Infrastructure: The government has earmarked ₹100 lakh crore (approximately $1.4 trillion) for infrastructure development under the National Infrastructure Pipeline (NIP).
- High-Speed Rail Network: Plans to expand the high-speed rail network to cover 8,000 km by 2029, with ongoing projects connecting major cities like Delhi, Mumbai, Chennai, and Kolkata.
- Economic Benefits: According to the NITI Aayog, the bullet train project is expected to generate over 36,000 direct and indirect jobs and boost the GDP of the regions it connects.

Statements from International Organisations:

- World Bank: "India's ambitious infrastructure plans, including the high-speed rail projects, are poised to transform its economy. By improving connectivity and urban infrastructure, India can achieve sustained economic growth and inclusive development."

- Asian Development Bank (ADB): "The modernisation of India's transportation infrastructure will enhance economic productivity and promote regional integration and environmental sustainability."

The Modi government's ambitious plans for high-speed rail and infrastructure revamp represent a transformative vision for India's future. By modernising transportation and urban infrastructure, the government aims to propel India towards becoming a developed nation by 2029. Despite challenges and criticisms, the visible transformations and global recognition underscore the potential of these initiatives to bring about lasting change. With continued investment, strategic planning, and commitment to sustainability, India is set to enhance its connectivity and economic growth, ensuring a brighter future for its citizens.

Uniform Civil Code

The Uniform Civil Code (UCC) proposes the establishment of a single set of laws governing personal matters for all citizens, regardless of religion. Envisioned in Article 44 of the Indian Constitution, the UCC aims to replace the personal laws based on the scriptures and customs of each major religious community in India with a common set of rules applicable to every citizen. The need for a UCC stems from the desire to promote national integration and ensure equality before the law.

Historical Context

The debate on personal laws and the need for a UCC dates back to the colonial era. The British colonial rulers codified personal laws based on religious scriptures and customs, which independent India later retained. The Constituent Assembly, while framing the Indian Constitution, included Article 44, which articulates the state's directive to endeavour to secure a UCC. However, due to political sensitivities, successive governments have hesitated to implement it.

Current Scenario

India's personal laws differ across religious communities, leading to disparities in issues such as marriage, divorce, inheritance, and adoption. For instance, while Hindu personal laws have undergone reforms, Muslim personal laws remain largely untouched. This inconsistency has led to judicial interventions, particularly in cases where personal laws conflict with fundamental rights.

Arguments in Favour of UCC

1. Gender Equality: The UCC is seen as a means to promote gender equality by removing discriminatory provisions in personal laws. For example, the practice of triple talaq in Muslim personal law was seen as unjust to women until it was banned by the Supreme Court in 2017.
2. Uniformity and Consistency: A common civil code would ensure uniformity in laws, providing a consistent legal framework for all citizens and reducing legal ambiguities.
3. National Integration: The UCC would promote national integration by fostering a sense of unity and reducing communal tensions based on personal laws.
4. Simplifying the Legal System: By eliminating the need for separate personal laws, a UCC would simplify the legal system, making it more accessible and less prone to litigation.

Arguments Against UCC

1. Religious Freedom: Critics argue that the UCC could infringe on religious freedoms by imposing a single set of laws on all communities, potentially disregarding their cultural and religious practices.
2. Cultural Diversity: India's rich cultural diversity necessitates the preservation of different personal laws, which reflect the customs and traditions of various communities.
3. Potential Backlash: Implementing the UCC could face significant resistance from religious communities, leading to social unrest.

Government's Stand and Efforts

Since taking office in 2014, Prime Minister Narendra Modi's government has consistently advocated for the UCC, positioning it as a key element of their reform agenda. Some of the notable steps taken include:

1. Law Commission's Recommendations: In 2018, the Law Commission of India was tasked with examining the feasibility of the UCC. Although it did not directly recommend a UCC, it suggested reforms to make personal laws more gender-just and non-discriminatory.
2. Judicial Interventions: The Modi government supported the Supreme Court's decisions in cases like the Shayara Bano case, which outlawed triple talaq. This was seen as a step towards implementing uniform principles in personal laws.
3. Public Consultations: Efforts have been made to engage with various stakeholders, including civil society organisations, to build consensus on the UCC. These consultations are crucial for addressing concerns and formulating an inclusive code.

Opposition's Perspective

Opposition parties have often resisted the UCC, arguing that it threatens religious freedoms and could disrupt the social fabric of the country. Critics within the opposition also accused the Modi government of using the UCC to further a majoritarian agenda. However, they have been criticised for not providing a clear alternative vision or engaging constructively in the debate.

Anecdotes from Other Nations to Provide a Comparative Analysis

Countries like France and Turkey have implemented uniform civil codes, leading to significant social reforms and modernisation. These examples illustrate that while challenging, the transition to a UCC can foster national unity and equality. In Turkey, adopting a civil code inspired by the Swiss Civil Code in 1926 was a pivotal step in the country's modernisation efforts.

Case Studies

1. Shah Bano case (1985): The Supreme Court's verdict in favour of Shah Bano, a Muslim woman seeking alimony, highlighted the need for a UCC. The subsequent political backlash and reversal through legislation underscored the complexities involved in personal law reform.
2. Triple Talaq Ban (2017): The Supreme Court's decision to ban instant triple talaq was a landmark ruling that addressed gender injustice within Muslim personal law. This case demonstrated judicial support for uniform principles across personal laws.

Public Opinion and Societal Impact

Surveys indicate mixed public opinion on the UCC, with a significant portion of the population supporting the idea of uniform laws, particularly in urban areas. Civil society organisations and activists have played a crucial role in advocating for the UCC, emphasising its potential to ensure gender justice and equality.

Future Prospects and Challenges

Implementing the UCC by 2029 requires a multifaceted approach:

1. Building Consensus: Engaging with all stakeholders to address concerns and build broad-based support is essential.
2. Phased Implementation: A gradual approach, starting with harmonising existing personal laws, can pave the way for a comprehensive UCC.

3. Educational Campaigns: Raising awareness about the benefits of the UCC and dispelling myths through public education campaigns.

The journey towards a Uniform Civil Code in India is fraught with challenges but holds the promise of fostering equality and national unity. The Modi government has taken significant steps towards this goal, but much remains to be done. Achieving a UCC by 2029 will require sustained efforts, inclusive dialogue, and a commitment to justice and equality for all citizens.

One Nation One Election

The concept of "One Nation, One Election" (ONOE) advocates for synchronising elections to the Lok Sabha (the lower house of India's parliament) and all state legislative assemblies, ideally conducting them simultaneously every five years. This proposal aims to reduce the frequent cycle of elections in India, which leads to significant economic and administrative disruptions. Since 2014, Prime Minister Narendra Modi and his government have been vocal proponents of ONOE, arguing that it is essential for the country's development and governance efficiency.

Historical Context

India conducted simultaneous elections for the Lok Sabha and state assemblies from 1952 to 1967. However, this synchronisation was disrupted due to premature dissolutions of certain state assemblies and the Lok Sabha. Since then, India has witnessed a perpetual cycle of elections, with some state or the other going to polls almost every year. This continuous election mode imposes a heavy burden on the exchequer, diverts government machinery from developmental work, and leads to policy paralysis due to the Model Code of Conduct being in place.

Arguments in Favour of One Nation, One Election

1. Cost Efficiency: Conducting simultaneous elections would significantly reduce the costs associated with deploying security

forces, transportation, and logistics, which are repeated for every election cycle.

2. Administrative Efficiency: Frequent elections disrupt the administration's focus on governance and developmental activities. A synchronised election schedule would allow for uninterrupted governance.
3. Policy Stability: The imposition of the Model Code of Conduct during elections restricts the announcement of new schemes and policies. Fewer elections would mean fewer interruptions in policy-making and implementation.
4. Voter Turnout and Engagement: Simultaneous elections could potentially increase voter turnout, as citizens can exercise their voting rights for both central and state governments on a single day.
5. Reducing Political Polarisation: Continuous campaigning contributes to a charged political environment. Fewer elections could help reduce the political acrimony and polarisation that often accompany frequent electoral contests.

Arguments Against One Nation, One Election

1. Federal Structure Concerns: Critics argue that simultaneous elections could undermine the federal structure of India by reducing the autonomy of states. They fear that national narratives might overshadow state issues during elections.
2. Logistical Challenges: Conducting elections across a vast and diverse country like India, with its logistical complexities, poses significant challenges. Ensuring the availability of sufficient Electronic Voting Machines (EVMs) and Voter-Verified Paper Audit Trail (VVPAT) systems is a logistical nightmare.

3. Emergency Scenarios: In case of a state government's premature dissolution, mechanisms would need to be in place to handle such scenarios without disrupting the synchronised election cycle.

Steps Taken by Modi Government Since 2014

1. Advocacy and Debate: Prime Minister Narendra Modi has repeatedly highlighted the need for ONOE in various forums, including parliamentary addresses and public speeches, to build a consensus on this issue.
2. NITI Aayog's Proposal: In 2017, NITI Aayog, the government's policy think tank, released a discussion paper advocating for ONOE. The paper outlined the benefits, challenges, and possible implementation strategies for simultaneous elections.
3. Law Commission Report: The 21st Law Commission, in its draft report in 2018, recommended holding simultaneous elections and provided a detailed framework for its implementation, including amendments to the Constitution and election laws.
4. Parliamentary Committee: A parliamentary committee was constituted to examine the feasibility of simultaneous elections. This committee has been engaging with various stakeholders to gather opinions and build a broader consensus.

Implementation Strategy

1. Constitutional Amendments: Implementing ONOE requires amending multiple articles of the Indian Constitution, including Articles 83, 85, 172, 174, and 356. This necessitates a two-thirds majority in both houses of parliament and ratification by at least half of the state legislatures.

2. Consensus Building: Achieving political consensus is crucial. It is imperative to engage with all political parties and stakeholders to address their concerns and build a common understanding.
3. Phased Implementation: A phased approach can be adopted, starting with aligning the election cycles of a few states with the Lok Sabha elections and gradually moving towards complete synchronisation.
4. Logistical Readiness: Ensuring the readiness of election machinery, including sufficient EVMs and VVPAT systems, is essential. Training and capacity building of election personnel are also crucial.
5. Legislative Framework: Introducing comprehensive electoral reforms to streamline the election process and address potential challenges arising from the synchronisation.

Anecdotes from several countries have successfully implemented synchronised elections to enhance governance efficiency:

1. South Africa: South Africa conducts simultaneous elections for its National Assembly and provincial legislatures. This system has helped streamline administrative processes and reduce election-related costs.
2. Indonesia: Indonesia holds simultaneous elections for its president and regional legislative bodies. This approach has improved voter turnout and reduced the frequency of election cycles.
3. Sweden: Sweden conducts elections for its national parliament, regional councils, and municipal councils simultaneously every four years, ensuring a stable and predictable electoral cycle.

Anecdote: Successful Implementation in Indonesia

Indonesia, with its vast geography and diverse population, faced challenges similar to India's in conducting frequent elections. By synchronising its presidential and regional legislative elections, Indonesia not only reduced electoral costs but also improved administrative efficiency and voter engagement. This reform has been widely recognised as a successful step towards enhancing democratic processes and governance.

Visible Transformation: Enhanced Governance and Stability

The implementation of ONOE would lead to significant improvements in governance and political stability in India. With fewer elections, the government can focus more on long-term developmental projects and policy initiatives without frequent interruptions. This would also foster a more conducive environment for economic growth and social development.

One Nation, One Election is a bold and transformative idea that has the potential to revolutionise India's electoral and governance landscape. The Modi government's advocacy for this reform underscores its commitment to efficient governance and national integration. While challenges exist, a phased and consensual approach can pave the way for its successful implementation by 2029. Learning from international examples and leveraging India's democratic strengths, ONOE can usher in a new era of political and economic stability in the country.

Opposition's Struggle

Since Narendra Modi assumed office as the Prime Minister of India in 2014, his government has maintained a stronghold over the country's political landscape. The BJP's remarkable victory in the 2014 general elections, followed by an even more substantial mandate in 2019, highlights the party's dominance. Despite the numerous challenges and controversies faced by the Modi administration, the opposition parties have struggled to present a unified and effective strategy to counter the BJP's influence.

The Opposition's Stagnation: 2014-2024

One of the most significant failures of the opposition parties, primarily led by the Indian National Congress (INC), has been their inability to form a cohesive front against the BJP. The fragmented nature of the opposition, with regional parties pursuing their own agendas, has led to a lack of a unified strategy. This disunity was starkly visible during the 2019 general elections when attempts to forge alliances fell apart, leading to scattered votes and a decisive victory for the BJP.

Ineffective Leadership and Vision

The leadership vacuum in the opposition has been another critical issue. The INC, historically the main rival to the BJP, has seen a decline in its leadership effectiveness. Despite his efforts, Rahul Gandhi has not been able to resonate with the masses as effectively as Narendra Modi. The opposition's messaging has often seemed reactive rather than proactive, lacking a clear and compelling vision for India's future.

Learning from the Past: BJP's Opposition Strategy (2004-2014)

Targeted Campaigns and Persistent Attacks

The BJP, during its time in opposition from 2004 to 2014, demonstrated a strategic and relentless approach to targeting the UPA government. Under the leadership of figures like Atal Bihari Vajpayee and later Narendra Modi, the BJP focused on key issues such as corruption, economic mismanagement, and national security. The BJP's campaign against the UPA was highlighted by the 'India Against Corruption' movement, which gained massive public support and highlighted the Congress-led government's vulnerabilities.

Effective Utilisation of Media and Communication

The BJP's strategic use of media and communication was another factor in its successful opposition role. Narendra Modi's speeches, both in the parliament and during public rallies, were designed to resonate with the common people. Modi's speech at the BJP's National Council Meeting in 2013, where he emphasised "Congress-mukt Bharat" (Congress-free India), became a rallying cry that unified the party's base and galvanised public sentiment.

The Path Forward: Lessons for Today's Opposition

Building a Unified Front

To effectively counter the BJP, the opposition parties must prioritise unity over regional ambitions. Forming strategic alliances and presenting a consolidated front can prevent vote fragmentation and create a formidable challenge to the BJP's dominance.

Strong Leadership and Clear Vision

The opposition needs strong, charismatic leaders who can articulate a clear and compelling vision for India's future. Learning from Modi's ability to connect with the masses, opposition leaders must work on crafting messages that resonate on a national level, addressing the aspirations and concerns of the people.

Strategic Use of Media and Communication

In an era dominated by digital and social media, the opposition must enhance its communication strategies. Effective use of media to highlight government failures, coupled with strong, fact-based narratives, can help in creating a counter-narrative to the BJP's dominance.

Global Example: Bringing Down a Strong Government Democratically

A notable example of a strong government being brought down by democratic means is the 2015 elections in Nigeria. The then-incumbent President Goodluck Jonathan, despite having a significant hold on power, was defeated by Muhammadu Buhari. This was largely due to a unified opposition under the All Progressives Congress (APC), which strategically highlighted issues such as corruption, economic mismanagement, and insecurity. The Nigerian opposition's success demonstrates the power of unity, strategic campaigning, and effective use of public sentiment in a democratic setup.

The opposition in India, if it continues on its current path, risks remaining ineffective against the Modi government's strategies. However, by learning from the BJP's past playbook and successful opposition movements worldwide, the opposition can reorient itself to pose a significant challenge. Unity, strong leadership, clear vision, and strategic communication are the pillars upon which a successful opposition strategy can be built, potentially altering the political landscape of India by 2029.

Synopsis

"In the Annals of Indian Political History: 2014-2029" is a comprehensive exploration of India's political landscape during this transformative period. Beginning with the government's visionary initiatives under the mantra of "Sabka Saath, Sabka Vikas," the narrative delves into key milestones such as the JAM initiative and expansion of LPG and electricity coverage. As the political landscape evolves, so does the government's mantra, evolving into "Sabka Sath, Sabka Vikas, Sabka Vishwas." The book explores significant policy decisions, including the abrogation of Article 370 and the Ayodhya dispute verdict, amidst fierce opposition and national debates. Looking ahead, it offers insights into the future trajectory of India, highlighting goals such as ending malnutrition and insurgency and empowering women. Through candid anecdotes and insightful analysis, the book captures the essence of a nation grappling with its past, navigating its present, and envisioning its future amidst a backdrop of political complexities and democratic experiments.

Epilogue

As we come to the end of our journey through the annals of Indian political history, we are reminded of the resilience, adaptability, and indomitable spirit that define our nation. The chapters preceding this epilogue have offered a panoramic view of the triumphs and tribulations, the highs and lows, that have shaped our collective destiny.

From the transformative reforms of the past to the bold aspirations for the future, India stands at a crossroads—a juncture where the echoes of the past reverberate with the promise of tomorrow. The path ahead is fraught with challenges, yet it is illuminated by the beacon of hope and possibility.

As we reflect on the pages turned, we are reminded of the power of democracy—the power to dream, dissent, and dialogue. In the cacophony of voices and the clash of ideologies lies the heartbeat of a vibrant democracy—a democracy that thrives on diversity, debate, and dissent.

In closing, let us remember that the story of India is not confined to the pages of history—it is a living, breathing narrative shaped by the dreams and aspirations of a billion souls. As we bid farewell to these pages, let us carry forward the lessons learned, cherished memories, and shared vision.

For in the tapestry of our nation's story, each thread represents a moment of triumph, a lesson learned, a hope renewed. And as we look towards the horizon, let us do so with optimism, determination, and a steadfast belief in the boundless potential of our beloved nation—India.

About the Author

Aditya Sharma is a finance professional currently working at a leading non-banking financial company (NBFC). With an MBA in Finance and multiple certifications, Aditya brings a wealth of knowledge and experience to the field. Recently, Aditya's debut book achieved the No. 1 spot on Amazon in its category, showcasing his expertise and insight. Now, with the release of his second book, Aditya continues to share his passion for finance and storytelling, aiming to inspire and educate readers around the world.

www.ingramcontent.com/pod-product-compliance
Lightning Source LLC
LaVergne TN
LVHW021159160826
845679LV00024B/2169

9798894465241